W9-CIP-570

The Illustrated
Book of Prayer

Poems, prayers and thoughts for every day

Publisher and Creative Director: Nick Wells
Project Editor and Picture Research: Emma Chafer
Special thanks to Laura Bulbeck and Esme Chapman

This edition first published 2014 by
FLAME TREE PUBLISHING
6 Melbray Mews
Fulham, London SW6 3NS
United Kingdom

www.flametreepublishing.com

18 17
7 9 10 8 6

© 2014 Flame Tree Publishing Ltd

ISBN 978-1-78361-109-6

A CIP record for this book is available from the British Library
upon request.

All rights reserved. No part of this publication may be reproduced,
stored in a retrieval system, or transmitted in any form or by any
means, electronic, mechanical, photocopying, recording or other-
wise, without prior permission in writing of the publisher.

Every effort has been made to contact copyright holders. In the event
of an oversight the publishers would be glad to rectify any omissions
in future editions of this book.

Printed in China

The Illustrated Book of Prayer

Poems, prayers and thoughts for every day

A special selection edited by E. I. Chafer

FLAME TREE PUBLISHING

Contents

Introduction 6

Thanks and Praise 10

Love and Forgiveness 46

Children's Prayers 86

Strength and Healing 124

Picture Credits and Acknowledgments .. 156

Index of Titles & Authors 158

Introduction

ince the beginning of civilisation, prayer has stood as a powerful pillar of hope binding together people of all backgrounds. Prayer has provided a common language in which to find solace, joy and truth. Its enduring use through the centuries is an absolute testament to the unwavering sanctity of its practice. Whether it is to fervently seek forgiveness, offer praise to a higher power or anything in between, prayer is called upon in an effort to connect with something beyond ourselves.

This anthology is a choice selection, although mainly Christian in origin, representing the myriad of sources of prayer; for prayers do not only find home in religious texts, but also in the hearts and minds of famed poets and inspired thinkers. From the archetypal, influential passages from the Bible and The Book Common of Prayer, to the eloquent flow of William Canton's (1845-1926) 'Through The Night Thy Angels Kept, the proliferation of prayer illuminates how, despite conflict and hardship, people have continually found gifts and happiness for which to offer thanks.

Through the words of Methodist brothers Charles and John Wesley (1703-91) (1707-88), prayer calls upon God for fortitude in the face

of adversity: in 'Messiah Prince of Peace!', Charles begs for peace; in 'Gentle Jesus, Meek And Mild', Charles and John pronounce God's ability to grant mercy.

The versatility and ease of prayer are also qualities that have contributed to its widespread devotion. The form of a prayer can be simple enough for a child to recite, yet retain its sacred meaning; such is the case with 'Now I lay me down to sleep'. However, a prayer can also be poetically effusive like 'Prayer at Sunrise' by James Weldon Johnson (1871–1938), which applauds the splendour of one of God's greatest bestowals: the sun.

Prayer through the medium of song offers an opportunity to honour God through music, as do the many prayer-hymns, some of which are featured in this collection, such as 'Glory Be To God On High' by Theodore Chickering Williams (1855–1915) and 'Rock of Ages' by Augustus Montague Toplady (1740–78).

Prayer offers comfort in its continued consistency; it refuses to fade from thought or practice. Featuring prayers from biblical times, through the middle ages, right up to the nineteenth century (including the work of Charles Dickens, 1812–70, and Oscar Wilde, 1854–1900), the twentieth century and the present day, this collection shows just how potent prayer remains.

Divided into four sections, the book journeys from the highest heights of adoration and worship to the passionate plea for the courage to endure in the most trying of times. Whether it is a prayer for love, or any impassioned supplication to a divine being, this anthology offers an engaging read, a chance to reaffirm your faith and an inspiration for reflection.

Thanks and Praise

A General Thanksgiving
The Book of Common Prayer, 1662 version

This to be said when any that have been prayed for desire to return praise.

ALMIGHTY God, Father of all mercies, we thine unworthy servants do give thee most humble and hearty thanks for all thy goodness and loving-kindness to us, and to all men; [*particularly to those who desire now to offer up their praises and thanksgivings for thy late mercies vouchsafed unto them.]

We bless thee for our creation, preservation, and all the blessings of this life; but above all, for thine inestimable love in the redemption of the world by our Lord Jesus Christ; for the means of grace, and for the hope of glory. And, we beseech thee, give us that due sense of all thy mercies, that our hearts may be unfeignedly thankful, and that we shew forth thy praise, not only with our lips, but in our lives; by giving up ourselves to thy service, and by walking before thee in holiness and righteousness all our days; through Jesus Christ our Lord, to whom with thee and the Holy Ghost be all honour and glory, world without end.

Amen.

At The Close Of The Year

John Newton (1725–1807)

Let hearts and tongues unite,
And loud thanksgivings raise:
'Tis duty, mingled with delight,
To sing the Saviour's praise.

To him we owe our breath,
He took us from the womb,
Which else had shut us up in death,
And prov'd an early tomb.

When on the breast we hung,
Our help was in the Lord;
'Twas he first taught our infant tongue
To form the lisping word.

When in our blood we lay,
He would not let us die,
Because his love had fix'd a day
To bring salvation nigh.

In childhood and in youth,
His eye was on us still:
Though strangers to his love and truth,
And prone to cross his will.

And since his name we knew,
How gracious has he been:
What dangers has he led us through,
What mercies have we seen!

Now through another year,
Supported by his care,
We raise our Ebenezer here,
'The Lord has help'd thus far'.

Our lot in future years
Unable to foresee,
He kindly, to prevent our fears,
Says, 'Leave it all to me'.

Yea, Lord, we wish to cast
Our cares upon thy breast!
Help us to praise thee for the past,
And trust thee for the rest.

For Success (extract)
Robert Louis Stevenson (1850–94)

Lord, behold our family here assembled.

We thank Thee for this place in which we dwell;

for the love that unites us;

for the peace accorded us this day;

for the hope with which we expect the morrow;

for the health, the work, the food, and the bright skies,
  that make our lives delightful;

for our friends in all parts of the earth, and our friendly
  helpers in this foreign isle.

Glory Be To God On High

Theodore Chickering Williams (1855–1915)

Glory be to God on high, Alleluia!
Let the whole creation cry, Alleluia!
Peace and blessing He has given, Alleluia!
Earth repeat the songs of heaven, Alleluia!

Creatures of the field and flood, Alleluia!
Earth and sea cry 'God is good', Alleluia!
Toiling pilgrims raise the song, Alleluia!
Saints in light the strain prolong, Alleluia!

Stars that have no voice to sing Alleluia!
Give their glory to our King, Alleluia!
Silent powers and angels' song, Alleluia!
All unto our God belong, Alleluia!

Doxology
Josephine Delphine Henderson Heard (1861 – 1921)

Great God accept our gratitude,
For the great gifts on us bestowed –
For raiment, shelter and for food.

Great God, our gratitude we bring,
Accept our humble offering,
For all the gifts on us bestowed,
Thy name be evermore adored.

Hail Father

Samuel Wesley, Jr. (1690–1739)

Hail, Father, whose creating call
Unnumbered worlds attend;
Jehovah, comprehending all,
Whom none can comprehend!

In light unsearchable enthroned,
Whom angels dimly see,
The fountain of the Godhead owned,
And foremost of the Three.

From Thee, through an eternal now,
The Son, Thine offspring, flowed;
An everlasting Father Thou,
An everlasting God.

Nor quite displayed to worlds above,
Nor quite on earth concealed;
By wondrous, unexhausted love,
To mortal man revealed.

Supreme and all-sufficient God,
When nature shall expire,
And worlds created by Thy nod
Shall perish by Thy fire.

Thy Name, Jehovah, be adored
By creatures without end,
Whom none but Thy essential Word
And Spirit comprehend.

Praise God From Whom All Blessings Flow

Thomas Ken (1637–1711)

Praise God from whom all blessings flow;
Praise Him, all creatures here below;
Praise Him above, ye Heavenly Hosts;
Praise Father, Son and Holy Ghost.

Amen.

The Song Of Moses
Exodus 15:1–18

I will sing to the Lord, for he has triumphed gloriously;
   horse and rider he has thrown into the sea.
The Lord is my strength and my might,
   and he has become my salvation;
this is my God, and I will praise him,
   my father's God, and I will exalt him.
The Lord is a warrior;
   the Lord is his name.

Pharaoh's chariots and his army he cast into the sea;
   his picked officers were sunk in the Red Sea.
The floods covered them;
   they went down into the depths like a stone.
Your right hand, O Lord, glorious in power –
   your right hand, O Lord, shattered the enemy
In the greatness of your majesty you overthrew
   your adversaries;
   you sent out your fury, it consumed them like stubble.
At the blast of your nostrils the waters piled up,
   the floods stood up in a heap;
   the deeps congealed in the heart of the sea.
The enemy said, 'I will pursue, I will overtake,
   I will divide the spoil, my desire shall have its fill of them.
   I will draw my sword, my hand shall destroy them'.

You blew with your wind, the sea covered them;
  they sank like lead in the mighty waters.

Who is like you, O Lord, among the gods?
  Who is like you, majestic in holiness,
  awesome in splendour, doing wonders?
You stretched out your right hand,
  the earth swallowed them.

In your steadfast love you led the people whom you redeemed;
  you guided them by your strength to your holy abode.
The peoples heard, they trembled;
  pangs seized the inhabitants of Philistia.
Then the chiefs of Edom were dismayed;
  trembling seized the leaders of Moab;
  all the inhabitants of Canaan melted away.

Terror and dread fell upon them;
  by the might of your arm they became as still as a stone
until your people, O Lord, passed by,
  until the people whom you acquired passed by.
You brought them in and planted them on the mountain of
  your own possession;
  the place, O Lord, that you made your abode,
  the sanctuary, O Lord, that your hands have established.
The Lord will reign forever and ever.

Traditional Prayer
(Author unknown)

Almighty God,
we thank you for the gift of your holy word.
May it be a lantern to our feet,
a light to our paths,
and a strength to our lives.
Take us and use us
to love and serve all men
in the power of the Holy Spirit
And in the name of your Son,
Jesus Christ our Lord.

All Lands Summoned To Praise God
Psalm 100

Make a joyful noise to the Lord all the earth.
Worship the Lord with gladness;
come into his presence with singing.

Know that the Lord is God.
It is he that made us and we are his;
we are his people, and the sheep of his pasture.

Enter his gates with thanksgiving,
and his courts with praise.
Give thanks to him, bless his name.

For the Lord is good;
his steadfast love endures forever,
and his faithfulness to all generations.

A Call To Worship And Obedience
Psalm 95

Come, let us sing for joy to the Lord;
   let us shout aloud to the Rock of our salvation.
Let us come before him with thanksgiving
   and extol him with music and song.
For the Lord is the great God,
   the great King above all gods.
In his hand are the depths of the earth,
   and the mountain peaks belong to him.
The sea is his, for he made it,
   and his hands formed the dry land.

Come, let us bow down in worship,
   let us kneel before the Lord our Maker;
for he is our God
   and we are the people of his pasture,
   the flock under his care.
Today, if you hear his voice,
   do not harden your hearts as you did at Meribah,
   as you did that day at Massah in the desert,
where your fathers tested and tried me,
   though they had seen what I did.
For forty years I was angry with that generation;
   I said, 'They are a people whose hearts go astray,
   and they have not known my ways'.
So I declared on oath in my anger,
   'They shall never enter my rest'.

Daniel Blesses God
Daniel 2:20–23

Blessed be the name of God from age to age,

for wisdom and power are his.

He changes times and seasons,

deposes kings and sets up kings;

he gives wisdom to the wise

and knowledge to those who have understanding.

He reveals deep and hidden things;

he knows what is in the darkness,

and light dwells with him.

To you, O God of my ancestors,

I give thanks and praise,

for you have given me wisdom and power,

and have now revealed to me what we asked of you,

for you have revealed to us what the king ordered.

Mary's Song Of Praise or The Magnificat

Luke 1:46–55

My soul exalts the Lord,
   And my spirit has rejoiced in God my Saviour.
For He has had regard for the humble state of His bondslave;
   For behold, from this time on all generations will count
   me blessed.
For the Mighty One has done great things for me;
   And holy is His name.
And His mercy is upon generation after generation
   toward those who fear Him.
He has done mighty deeds with His arm;
   He has scattered those who were proud in the thoughts
   of their heart.
He has brought down rulers from their thrones,
   And has exalted those who were humble.
He has filled the hungry with good things;
   And sent away the rich empty-handed.
He has given help to Israel His servant,
   In remembrance of His mercy,
As He spoke to our fathers,
   To Abraham and his descendants forever.

Praise The Judge Of The World

Psalm 98

O sing to the Lord a new song,

    For He has done wonderful things,

His right hand and His holy arm have gained the victory for Him.

The Lord has made known His salvation;

    He has revealed His righteousness in the sight of the nations.

He has remembered His loving kindness and His faithfulness

    to the house of Israel;

All the ends of the earth have seen the salvation of our God.

Shout joyfully to the Lord, all the earth;

    Break forth and sing for joy and sing praises.

Sing praises to the Lord with the lyre,

    With the lyre and the sound of melody.

With trumpets and the sound of the horn

    Shout joyfully before the King, the Lord.

Let the sea roar and all it contains,

    The world and those who dwell in it.

Let the rivers clap their hands,

    Let the mountains sing together for joy

Before the Lord, for He is coming to judge the earth;

He will judge the world with righteousness

    And the peoples with equity.

Prayer Of St Richard
Saint Richard of Chichester (1197–1253)

Thanks be to Thee, my Lord Jesus Christ

For all the benefits Thou hast given me,

For all the pains and insults Thou hast borne for me.

O most merciful Redeemer, friend and brother,

May I know Thee more clearly,

Love Thee more dearly,

Follow Thee more nearly.

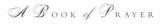

Thanksgiving For Plenty
The Book of Common Prayer, 1662 version

O MOST merciful Father, who of thy gracious goodness hast heard the devout prayers of thy Church, and turned our dearth and scarcity into cheapness and plenty:

We give thee humble thanks for this thy special bounty; beseeching thee to continue thy loving-kindness unto us, that our land may yield us her fruits of increase, to thy glory and our comfort; through Jesus Christ our Lord.

Amen.

To God Who Gives Our Daily Bread
Thomas Tallis (c. 1510–85)

To God who gives our daily bread
A thankful song we raise,
And pray that he who sends us food
May fill our hearts with praise.

Love and Forgiveness

A Confession For Morning Prayer
The Book of Common Prayer, 1662

Almighty and most merciful Father,

We have erred, and strayed from thy ways like lost sheep,

We have followed too much the devices and desires

  of our own hearts,

We have offended against thy holy laws,

We have left undone those things which we ought to

  have done,

And we have done those things which we

  ought not to have done,

And there is no health in us:

But thou, O Lord, have mercy upon us, miserable offenders;

Spare thou them, O God, which confess their faults.

Restore thou them that are penitent;

According to thy promises declared unto mankind in

  Christ Jesu our Lord:

And grant, O most merciful Father, for his sake,

That we may hereafter live a godly, righteous, and sober life,

To the glory of thy holy Name.

Amen.

Penitence

Adapted extract from The Consolation,
by Edward Young (1683 – 1765)

Great God!

Greater than Greatest! Better than the best!

Kinder than kindest! With soft pity's eye,

... Look down – down – down,

On a poor breathing particle in dust!

Or, lower, – an immortal in his crimes.

His crimes forgive! Forgive his virtues, too!

Those smaller faults, half-converts to the right.

A Prayer
George MacDonald (1824–1905)

When I look back upon my life nigh spent,
Nigh spent, although the stream as yet flows on,
I more of follies than of sins repent,
Less for offence than Love's shortcomings moan.
With self, O Father, leave me not alone –
Leave not with the beguiler the beguiled;
Besmirched and ragged, Lord, take back thine own:
A fool I bring thee to be made a child.

A Complaint Of A Sinner

Humfrey Gifford (1550–1600)

O Lord most deare, [with] many a teare, lamenting, lame[n]ting,
  I fall before thy face,
And for e[a]ch crime, done ere this time, repenting, repenting
  Most humbly call for grace.
Through wanton will, I must confesse,
Thy precepts still I doe transgresse,
The world with his vayne pleasure,
Bewitcht my senses so,
That I could find no leasure,
  My vices to forgoe.
I graunt I haue through my deserte,
Deserud great plagues and bitter smart.

But yet sweet God, doe stay thy rod, forgeue me, forgeue me,
  Which doe thine ayde implore,
O cease thine ire, I thee desire, beleeue me, beleue me,
  I will so sinne no more.
But still shall pray thy holy name,
  In the right way my steppes to frame,
So shall I not displease thee,
  Which art my Lord of might.
My heart and tongue shall prayse thee,
  Most humbly day and night.
I will delight continually,
  Thy name to lawde and magnify.

With sighes & sobs, my heart it throbs, remembring, remembring
   The fraylty of my youth,
I ran a race, deuoyd of grace, not rendring, not rendring
   Due reuerence to thy truth.
Such care I cast on earthly toyes,
   That nought I past for heauenly ioyes,
But now it me repenteth,
   My heart doeth bleede for woe,
Which inwardly lamenteth,
   That euer it sinned so.
With many a sigh, and many a grone,
   O Lord to thee I make my mone.

Though furious fires of fond desires, allure me, allure me,
   From thee so wander wyde:
Let pitifull eyes, and moystened eyes, procure thee, procure thee
   To be my Lorde and guyde.
As Scripture sayth, thou doest not craue,
   A sinners death, but wouldest him saue:
That sinfull wretch am I O Lorde,
   Which would repent and liue,
With ceaslesse plaints I cry Lorde,
   Thy pardon to me geue.
O Lord for thy sweete Iesu sake,
   Doe not shut up thy mercie gate.

Mercy, mercy, mercy, graunt me I pray thee, I pray thee,
   Graunt mercy louing Lorde,
Let not the Diuel which meanes me euill, betray me, betray mee,
   Protect me with thy worde.
So shall my heart find sweete reliefe,
   Which now feeles smart and bitter griefe,
O Lord, I doe request thee,
   To guyde my steppes so well,
That when death shall arest me,
   My soule with thee may dwell
In heauen aboue, where Angels sing,
   Continuall prayse, to thee theyr king.

A Hymn To God The Father
John Donne (1572–1631)

Wilt thou forgive that sin where I begun,

Which was my sin, though it were done before?

Wilt thou forgive that sin, through which I run,

And do run still: though still I do deplore?

When thou hast done, thou hast not done,

For I have more.

Wilt thou forgive that sin which I have won

Others to sin? and made my sin their door?

Wilt thou forgive that sin which I did shun

A year, or two, but wallow'd in, a score?

When thou hast done, thou hast not done,

For I have more.

I have a sin of fear, that when I have spun

My last thread, I shall perish on the shore

But swear by thyself, that at my death thy Son

Shall shine as he shines now, and heretofore;

And, having done that, thou hast done,

I fear no more.

Prayer For Cleansing And Pardon
Psalm 51, Attr. King David (1040 bc–970 bc)

Have mercy on me, O God,
  according to your unfailing love;
according to your great compassion
  blot out my transgressions.
Wash away all my iniquity
  and cleanse me from my sin.

For I know my transgressions,
  and my sin is always before me.
Against you, you only, have I sinned
  and done what is evil in your sight,
so that you are proved right when you speak
  and justified when you judge.
Surely I was sinful at birth,
  sinful from the time my mother conceived me.

Surely you desire truth in the inner parts;
  you teach me wisdom in the inmost place.
Cleanse me with hyssop, and I will be clean;
  wash me, and I will be whiter than snow.
Let me hear joy and gladness;
  let the bones you have crushed rejoice.
Hide your face from my sins
  and blot out all my iniquity.

Create in me a pure heart, O God,
  and renew a steadfast spirit within me.
Do not cast me from your presence
  or take your Holy Spirit from me.
Restore to me the joy of your salvation
  and grant me a willing spirit, to sustain me.
Then I will teach transgressors your ways,
  and sinners will turn back to you.
Save me from bloodguilt, O God,
    the God who saves me,
    and my tongue will sing of your righteousness.

O Lord, open my lips,
  and my mouth will declare your praise.
You do not delight in sacrifice, or I would bring it;
  you do not take pleasure in burnt offerings.
The sacrifices of God are a broken spirit;
  a broken and contrite heart,
    O God, you will not despise.

In your good pleasure make Zion prosper;
  build up the walls of Jerusalem.
Then there will be righteous sacrifices,
  whole burnt offerings to delight you;
    then bulls will be offered on your altar.

Prayer For Forgiveness Of Sins
Saint Gemma Galgani (1878–1903)

My Jesus, I place all my sins before you.

In my estimation

They do not deserve pardon,

But I ask you

To close your eyes

To my want of merit

And open them

To your infinite merit.

Since you willed

To die for my sins,

Grant me forgiveness

For all of them.

Thus, I may no longer feel

The burden of my sins,

A burden that oppresses me

Beyond measure.

Assist me, dear Jesus,

For I desire to become good

No matter what the cost

Take away, destroy,

And utterly root out

Whatever you find in me

That is contrary

To your holy will.

At the same time, dear Jesus, illumine me

So that I may walk in your holy light.

Rock Of Ages
Augustus Montague Toplady (1740 – 78)

Rock of Ages, cleft for me,
Let me hide myself in Thee;
Let the water and the blood,
From Thy wounded side which flowed,
Be of sin the double cure;
Save from wrath and make me pure.

Not the labour of my hands
Can fulfil Thy law's demands;
Could my zeal no respite know,
Could my tears forever flow,
All for sin could not atone;
Thou must save, and Thou alone.

Nothing in my hand I bring,
Simply to the cross I cling;
Naked, come to Thee for dress;
Helpless look to Thee for grace;
Foul, I to the fountain fly;
Wash me, Saviour, or I die.

While I draw this fleeting breath,
When my eye-strings break in death,
When I soar to worlds unknown,
See Thee on Thy judgment throne,
Rock of Ages, cleft for me,
Let me hide myself in Thee.

Pax Christi Daily Prayer
Pax Christi International Catholic Movement for Peace

Thank you loving God
For the gift of life
For this wonderful world which we all share
For the joy of love and friendship
For the challenge of helping to build
  your kingdom.

Strengthen
My determination to work for a world of peace and justice
My conviction that, whatever our nationality or race, we are all
  global citizens, one in Christ
My courage to challenge the powerful with the values of the Gospel
My commitment to find nonviolent ways of resolving conflict –
  personal, local, national and international
My efforts to forgive injuries and to love those
I find it hard to love.

Teach me
To share the gifts you have given me
To speak out for the victims of injustice who have no voice
To reject the violence which runs through much of our world today.

Holy Spirit of God
Renew my hope for a world free from the cruelty and evil of war
  so that we may all come to share in God's peace and justice.

Amen.

Hush, All Ye Sounds Of War
William H. Draper (1855–1933)

Hush, all ye sounds of war, ye nations all be still,
A voice of heav'nly joy steals over vale and hill,
O hear the angels sing the captive world's release,
This day is born in Bethlehem the Prince of Peace.

No more divided be, ye families of men,
Old enmity forget, old friendship knit again,
In the new year of God let brothers' love increase,
This day is born in Bethlehem the Prince of Peace.

Turn Our Hearts
Philip Melanchthon (1497–1560)

To you, O Son of God, Lord Jesus Christ,
as you pray to the eternal Father,
we pray, make us one in him.
Lighten our personal distress
and that of our society.
Receive us into the fellowship
of those who believe.
Turn our hearts, O Christ,
to truth everlasting
and healing harmony.

To Do Our Part
Author unknown, Japanese

God our Father, Creator of the world,
please help us to love one another.
Make nations friendly with other nations;
make all of us love one another like brothers and sisters.
Help us to do our part to bring peace in the world
and happiness to all people.

The Collect For Saint Stephen's Day
The Book of Common Prayer, 1662 version

GRANT, O Lord, that, in all our sufferings here upon earth, for the testimony of thy truth, we may stedfastly [sic] look up to heaven, and by faith behold the glory that shall be revealed; and, being filled with the Holy Ghost, may learn to love and bless our persecutors, by the example of thy first Martyr Saint Stephen, who prayed for his murderers to thee, O blessed Jesus, who standest at the right hand of God to succour all those that suffer for thee, our only Mediator and Advocate.

Amen.

An Interfaith Prayer For Peace
Author unknown, Pax Christi

O God, you are the source of life and peace.

Praised be your name forever.

We know it is you who turn our minds to thoughts of peace.

Hear our prayer in this time of crisis.

Your power changes hearts

Muslims, Christians and Jews remember, and profoundly affirm,

That they are followers of the one God,

Children of Abraham, brothers and sisters;

Enemies begin to speak to one another;

those who were estranged join hands in friendship;

nations seek the way of peace together.

Strengthen our resolve to give witness to these

truths by the way we live.

Give to us:

Understanding that puts an end to strife;

Mercy that quenches hatred, and

Forgiveness that overcomes vengeance.

Empower all people to live in your law of love

Amen.

O God Of Love, O King Of Peace
Henry Williams Baker (1821-77)

O God of love, O King of Peace,
Make wars throughout the world to cease;
The wrath of sinful men restrain,
Give peace, O God, give peace again!

Remember, Lord, Thy works of old,
The wonders that our fathers told;
Remember not our sin's dark stain,
Give peace, O God, give peace again!

Whom shall we trust but Thee, O Lord?
Where rest but on Thy faithful Word?
None ever called on Thee in vain,
Give peace, O God, give peace again!

Where saints and angels dwell above,
All hearts are knit in holy love;
O bind us in that heavenly chain!
Give peace, O God, give peace again!

Collect For Love
Brooke Foss Westcott (1825–1901)

Almighty and most merciful Father, Who hast given us
a new commandment that we should love one an-
other, give us also grace that we may fulfil it. Make us
gentle, courteous, and forbearing. Direct our lives, so
that we may look each to the good of others in word
and deed. And hallow all our friendships by the bless-
ing of Thy Spirit, for His sake, who loved us and gave
Himself for us, JESUS CHRIST our Lord.

Amen.

Messiah, Prince Of Peace!

John and Charles Wesley (1703–91 and 1707–88)

Messiah, Prince of peace!
Where men each other tear,
Where war is learned, they must confess,
Thy kingdom is not there.
Who, prompted by Thy foe,
Delight in human blood,
Apollyon is their king, we know,
And Satan is their god.

But shall he still devour
The souls redeemed by Thee?
Jesus, stir up Thy glorious power
And end the apostasy!
Come, Saviour, from above,
O'er all our hearts to reign;
And plant the kingdom of Thy love

In every heart of man.
Then shall we exercise
The hellish art no more,
While Thou our long-lost paradise
Dost with Thyself restore.
Fightings and wars shall cease,
And, in Thy Spirit giv'n,
Pure joy and everlasting peace
Shall turn our earth to Heav'n.

The Collect for Ash Wednesday
The Book of Common Prayer, 1662

ALMIGHTY and everlasting God, who hatest nothing
that thou hast made and dost forgive the sins of all
them that are penitent:

Create and make in us new and contrite hearts, that
we, worthily lamenting our sins, and acknowledging
our wretchedness, may obtain of thee, the God of all
mercy, perfect remission and forgiveness; through
Jesus Christ our Lord.

Amen.

Children's
Prayers

A Child's Hymn
Charles Dickens (1812–70)

Hear my prayer, O heavenly Father,
Ere I lay me down to sleep;
Bid Thy angels, pure and holy,
Round my bed their vigil keep.

My sins are heavy, but Thy mercy
Far outweighs them, every one;
Down before Thy cross I cast them,
Trusting in Thy help alone.

Keep me through this night of peril
Underneath its boundless shade;
Take me to Thy rest, I pray Thee,
When my pilgrimage is made.

None shall measure out Thy patience
By the span of human thought;
None shall bound the tender mercies
Which Thy Holy Son has bought.

Pardon all my past transgressions,
Give me strength for days to come;
Guide and guard me with Thy blessing
Till Thy angels bid me home.

Now I Lay Me Down To Sleep

Author unknown, 17th century

Now I lay me down to sleep,
I pray thee, Lord, my soul to keep;
If I should die before I wake,
I pray thee, Lord, my soul to take.

Matthew, Mark, Luke And John
Author unknown, traditional

Matthew, Mark, Luke and John,
Bless the bed that I lie on.
Four corners to my bed,
Four angels round my head;
One to watch and one to pray
And two to bear my soul away.

Good-night Prayer For A Little Child
Henry Johnstone, pre-1907

Father, unto Thee I pray,
Thou hast guarded me all day;
Safe I am while in Thy sight,
Safely let me sleep to-night.

Bless my friends, the whole world bless,
Help me to learn helpfulness;
Keep me ever in Thy sight:
So to all I say Good-night.

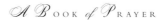

Child's Evening Hymn
Sabine Baring-Gould (1834–1924)

Now the day is over,
Night is drawing nigh,
Shadows of the evening
Steal across the sky.

Now the darkness gathers,
Stars begin to peep,
Birds and beasts and flowers
Soon will be asleep.

Jesu, give the weary
Calm and sweet repose;
With thy tenderest blessing
May our eyelids close.

Grant to little children
Visions bright of thee;
Guard the sailors tossing
On the deep blue sea.

Comfort every sufferer
Watching late in pain;
Those who plan some evil
From their sin restrain.

Through the long night-watches
May thine angels spread
Their white wings above me,
Watching round my bed.

When the morning wakens,
Then may I arise
Pure and fresh and sinless
In thy holy eyes.

Glory to the Father,
Glory to the Son,
And to thee, bless'd Spirit,
Whilst all ages run.

Amen.

Through The Night Thy Angels Kept
William Canton (1845–1926)

Through the night Thy angels kept
Watch beside me while I slept;
Now the dark has passed away,
Thank Thee, Lord, for this new day.

North and south and east and west
May Thy holy Name be blest;
Everywhere beneath the sun,
As in Heaven, Thy will be done.

Give me food that I may live;
Every naughtiness forgive;
Keep all evil things away
From Thy little child this day.

Jesus, Friend Of Little Children
Walter John Mathams (1853 – 1931)

Jesus, Friend of little children,
Be a friend to me;
Take my hand, and ever keep me
Close to Thee.

Teach me how to grow in goodness,
Daily as I grow;
Thou hast been a child, and surely
Thou dost know.

Step by step O lead me onward,
Upward into youth;
Wiser, stronger, still becoming
In Thy truth.

Never leave me, nor forsake me;
Ever be my friend;
For I need Thee, from life's dawning
To its end.

Refrain From 'Jesus Loves The Little Children'

Clare Herbert Woolston (1856–1927)

Jesus loves the little children,
All the children of the world.
Red and yellow, black and white,
All are precious in his sight,
Jesus loves the little children of the world.

Gentle Jesus, Meek And Mild
Charles Wesley (1707–88)

Gentle Jesus, meek and mild,
Look upon a little child;
Pity my simplicity,
Suffer me to come to Thee.

Fain I would to Thee be brought,
Dearest God, forbid it not;
Give me, dearest God, a place
In the kingdom of Thy grace.

Lamb of God, I look to Thee;
Thou shalt my Example be;
Thou art gentle, meek, and mild;
Thou wast once a little child.

Fain I would be as Thou art;
Give me Thine obedient heart;
Thou art pitiful and kind,
Let me have Thy loving mind.

Let me, above all, fulfil
God my heav'nly Father's will;
Never His good Spirit grieve;
Only to His glory live.

Thou didst live to God alone;
Thou didst never seek Thine own;
Thou Thyself didst never please:
God was all Thy happiness.

Loving Jesus, gentle Lamb,
In Thy gracious hands I am;
Make me, Saviour, what Thou art,
Live Thyself within my heart.

I shall then show forth Thy praise,
Serve Thee all my happy days;
Then the world shall always see
Christ, the holy Child, in me.

A Simple Thanksgiving Prayer
Ralph Waldo Emerson (1803–82)

For each new morning with its light,
For rest and shelter of the night,
For health and food, for love and friends,
For everything Thy goodness sends.

Be Near Me, Lord Jesus

John McFarland

Be near me, Lord Jesus,
  I ask Thee to stay
Close by me forever,
  and love me, I pray.
Bless all the dear children
  in thy tender care,
And fit us for heaven,
  to live with Thee there.

The third stanza from Away in A Manger.
First printed in 1892, probably by
Charles Hutchinson Gabriel (1856–1932)

Jesus Loves Me
Anna Bartlett Warner (1827–1915)

Jesus loves me – this I know,

For the Bible tells me so,

Little ones to Him belong,

They are weak but He is strong.

Yes, Jesus loves me.

Yes, Jesus loves me.

Yes, Jesus loves me. The Bible tells me so.

Lead Us, Heavenly Father

Brooke Herford (d. c. 1903)

Lead us, heavenly Father,
In our opening way,
Lead us in the morning
Of our little day.
While our hearts are happy,
While our souls are free,
May we give our childhood
As a song to Thee.

Lead us, heavenly Father,
As the way grows long,
Be our strong salvation,
Be our joyous song.
Gladdened by Thy mercies,
Chastened by Thy rod,
May we walk through all things
Humbly with our God.

Lead us, heavenly Father,
By Thy voices clear –
Through Thy prophets holy,
Through Thy Son so dear –
Him Who took the children
In His arms of love;
May we all be gathered
In His home above.

Father In Heaven
Kate Douglas Wiggin (1856—1923)

Father in heaven,

Help Thy little children

To love and serve Thee

Throughout this day.

Help us to be truthful

Help us to be kindly.

That we may please Thee

In all we do or say.

Amen.

Child's Grace

Edith Rutter Leatham (19th–20th century)

Thank you God for the world so sweet,
Thank you for the food we eat,
Thank you for the birds that sing
Thank you, God, for everything!

Lord And Saviour, True And Kind
Handley Carr Glynn Moule (1841–1920)

Lord and Saviour, true and kind,
Be the Master of my mind;
Bless, and guide, and strengthen still
All my powers of thought and will.

While I ply the scholar's task,
Jesus Christ, be near, I ask;
Help the memory, clear the brain,
Knowledge still to seek and gain.

Here I train for life's swift race;
Let me do it in Thy grace;
Here I arm me for life's fight;
Let me do it in Thy might.

Thou hast made me mind and soul;
I for Thee would use the whole;
Thou hast died that I might live;
All my powers to Thee I give.

Striving, thinking, learning, still,
Let me follow thus Thy will,
Till my whole glad nature be
Trained for duty and for Thee.

Strength
& Healing

The Lord's Prayer
Based on The Book of Matthew, 6:9-13

Our Father, who art in heaven,

Hallowed be thy Name.

Thy kingdom come.

Thy will be done,

On earth as it is in heaven.

Give us this day our daily bread.

And forgive us our trespasses,

And we forgive those who trespass against us.

And leave us not into temptation,

But deliver us from evil.

From thine is the kingdom,

and the power, and the glory,

for ever and ever.

Amen

The Third Collect, For Grace (Morning Prayer)

The Book of Common Prayer, 1662 version

O LORD our heavenly Father, Almighty and everlasting God, who hast safely brought us to the beginning of this day:

Defend us in the same with thy mighty power; and grant that this day we fall into no sin, neither run into any kind of danger; but that all our doings being ordered by thy governance, to do always that is righteous in thy sight; through Jesus Christ our Lord.

Amen.

The Divine Shepherd
Psalm 23, Attr. King David (1040 bc–970 bc)

The Lord is my shepherd, I shall not be in want.
  He makes me lie down in green pastures,
he leads me beside quiet waters,
  he restores my soul.
He guides me in paths of righteousness
  for his name's sake.

Even though I walk
  through the valley of the shadow of death,
  I will fear no evil,
for you are with me;
  your rod and your staff,
  they comfort me.

You prepare a table before me
  in the presence of my enemies.
You anoint my head with oil;
  my cup overflows.
Surely goodness and love will follow me
  all the days of my life,
and I will dwell in the house of the Lord
  forever.

O Lord My God, Receive My Prayer

Mary Stuart (1542–87)

O Lord my God, receive my prayer
Which is according to thy holy will;
For if, O great king, it should please thee still
I shall defend thee while I still draw air.
Alas, O Lord, I shall backslide once more,
Fatigued too soon unless thy bounty fill
And give resolve unto my own weak will
And with thy virtue open wide the door.
You wish, Lord, to be master of my heart.
Come then O Lord and make me your redoubt
That earthly love and hate be driven out
And good and evil and all care depart.
Only allow me to draw near to you,
Repentant, constant in my faith and true.

Psalm Of Protection (extract)

Extract from Psalm 27: 1-3,
Attr. King David (1040 bc-970 bc)

The Lord is my light and my salvation –
whom shall I fear?
The Lord is the stronghold of my life –
of whom shall I be afraid?
When evil men advance against me
to devour my flesh,
when my enemies and my foes attack me,
they will stumble and fall.
Though an army besiege me,
my heart will not fear;
though war break out against me,
even then will I be confident.

Evening Prayer (extract)
Jane Austen (1775–1817)

Father of Heaven! whose goodness has brought us in safety to the close of this day, dispose our hearts in fervent prayer. Another day is now gone, and added to those, for which we were before accountable. Teach us almighty father, to consider this solemn truth, as we should do, that we may feel the importance of every day, and every hour as it passes, and earnestly strive to make a better use of what thy goodness may yet bestow on us, than we have done of the time past.

Give us grace to endeavour after a truly Christian spirit to seek to attain that temper of forbearance and patience of which our blessed saviour has set us the highest example; and which, while it prepares us for the spiritual happiness of the life to come, will secure to us the best enjoyment of what this world can give. Incline us oh God! to think humbly of ourselves, to be severe only in the examination of our own conduct, to consider our fellow-creatures with kindness, and to judge of all they say and do with that charity which we would desire from them ourselves.

Prayer At Sunrise
James Weldon Johnson (1871–1938)

O mighty, powerful, dark-dispelling sun,
Now thou art risen, and thy day begun.
How shrink the shrouding mists before thy face,
As up thou spring'st to thy diurnal race!
How darkness chases darkness to the west,
As shades of light on light rise radiant from thy crest!
For thee, great source of strength, emblem of might,
In hours of darkest gloom there is no night.
Thou shinest on though clouds hide thee from sight,
And through each break thou sendest down thy light.

O greater Maker of this Thy great sun,
Give me the strength this one day's race to run,
Fill me with light, fill me with sun-like strength,
Fill me with joy to rob the day its length.
Light from within, light that will outward shine,
Strength to make strong some weaker heart than mine,
Joy to make glad each soul that feels its touch;
Great Father of the sun, I ask this much.

Celtic Prayer
Author unknown

O God, listen to my prayer
Let my earnest petition come to you,
For I know that you are hearing me
As surely as though I saw you with mine eyes.

I am placing a lock upon my heart,
I am placing a lock upon my thoughts,
I am placing a lock upon my lips
And double-knitting them.

Aught that is amiss for my soul
In the pulsing of my death,
May you, O God, sweep it from me
And may you shield me in the blood of your love.

Let no thought come to my heart,

Let no sound come to my ear,

Let no temptation come to my eye,

Let no fragrance come to my nose,

Let no fancy come to my mind,

Let no ruffle come to my spirit,

That is hurtful to my poor body this night,

Nor ill for my soul at the hour of my death;

But may you yourself, O God of life,

Be at my breast, be at my back,

You to me as a star, you to me as a guide,

From my life's beginning to my life's closing.

A Heart
Eberhard Arnold (1883–1935)

Give me a heart, dear heavenly Father,
a heart that's free of all self-will,
a heart obedient to thy counsel,
that gladly thy commands fulfils.

Give me a heart prepared to practise
true self-denial at any time,
a heart that loves its enemies,
assured of glories yet to come.

Give me a heart of sympathy
for every person mired in sin,
that guides them toward the Father's land,
embraces them, and takes them in.

Give me a heart that hankers not
for worldly pleasures, selfish ends,
a heart that loves the poor, and so
forgets itself, a hand to lend.

Give me a heart that pays no heed
to threats or scorn or ridicule,
that keeps faith always with its God,
though blamed, despised, or called a fool.

A heart like thine, that lives for God –
would such a heart be given to me!
O Jesus, take me and all my gifts:
I'll find this heart alone in thee.